Drawing
&
...d

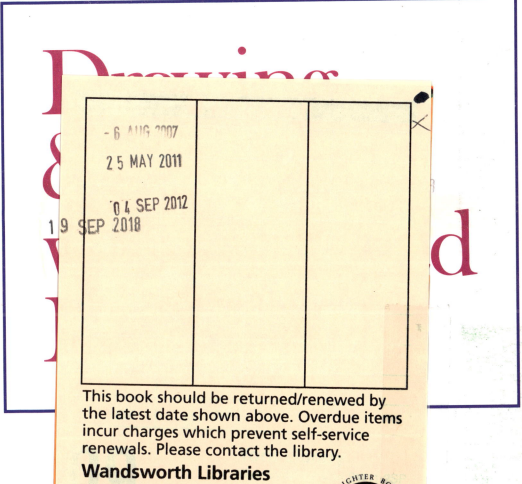

Sterling Publishing Co., Inc. New York

Library of Congress Cataloging-in-Publication Data

Birker, Stefan.
    [Zeichnen und malen mit Buntstiften. English]
    Drawing & painting with colored pencils / Stefan Birker.
        p.   cm.
    Includes index.
    Summary: Describes techniques and provides exercises for drawing
with pencils and colored pencils and also for using oil pastels.
    ISBN 0-8069-0312-0
    1. Colored pencil drawing—Technique—Juvenile literature.
2. Pastel drawing—Technique—Juvenile literature.   [1. Colored
pencil drawing—Technique.   2. Pastel drawing—Technique.
3. Drawing—Technique.]   I. Title.   II. Title: Drawing and painting
with colored pencils.
NC892.B5713   1993
741.2′4—dc20
                                     92-41349
                                        CIP
                                        AC

Translated by Elisabeth E. Reinersmann

Library of Congress Cataloging-in-Publication Data

10 9 8 7 6 5 4 3 2 1

Published 1993 by Sterling Publishing Company, Inc.
387 Park Avenue South, New York, N.Y. 10016
Originally published by Augustus Verlag, Augsburg
under the title *Zeichnen und Malen mit Buntstiften*
© 1990 by Weltbild Verlag, GmbH
English translation © 1993 by Sterling Publishing Inc.
Distributed in Canada by Sterling Publishing
% Canadian Manda Group, P.O. Box 920, Station U
Toronto, Ontario, Canada M8Z 5P9
Distributed in Great Britain and Europe by Cassell PLC
Villiers House, 41/47 Strand, London WC2N 5JE, England
Distributed in Australia by Capricorn Link Ltd.
P.O. Box 665, Lane Cove, NSW 2066
Printed and bound in Hong Kong
All rights reserved

Sterling ISBN 0-8069-0312-0

Introduction

Houses in Brittany

This book describes in detail techniques for drawing and painting with colored pencils. Individual exercises are systematically arranged and accompanied by numerous examples that are meant to steer the imagination. The text that goes along with the drawings, on the one hand, discusses the techniques and materials that are used and, on the other hand, the problems and issues involved in the creative process.

The book not only deals with the use of colored pencils but also touches on the many different effects that can be achieved when colored pencils are combined with other materials, like soft-tipped pens and oil pastels. However, the main focus of the book is on colored pencils. They are very similar to ordinary pencils, except that their center consists of a colored material instead of graphite. Handling a colored pencil is not unlike handling a graphite pencil.

Therefore, start by using colored pencils just as you would ordinary pencils, and do not use any other implements, like cloth for wiping or water; even the eraser is taboo. Instead, experiment with the various brands of colored pencils on the market and all the different types of drawing surface that are available and see what kinds of effect you can create.

Hurdle Race

Furthermore, do not force trying to find your "own" style. You already have your own style, which has existed in your subconscious since you were a child.

The development of your style will take place simply by the repeated act of drawing. Trying to imitate somebody else's style would only hinder your artistic development; at best, you would become a copier.

Consequently, the examples presented in this book are only meant to serve as an inspiration; their function is to illustrate, to open up new possibilities and point you in new directions. The overriding emphasis here is not to teach you how particular artists draw but to expose you to their techniques so that you can incorporate them into your own repertoire.

This book can be used by people at many different levels: art students, professionals, and all those who pursue drawing and painting as a hobby.

Contents

What Is a Drawing?

Obviously, a drawing is a drawing; however, colored-pencil drawings have characteristics all their own. While, in general, it is the *line* that gives expression to a drawing, it is the *color* of the colored pencil that adds to the drawing's overall impact. This is, of course, also true for pastel and oil-pastel drawings, but their strokes are broad and more painterly. In contrast, colored-pencil drawings generally have thinner and stronger lines; therefore, they can be said to be more closely related to pencil drawings.

The basic difference between a drawing and a painting is not the color but that in a painting planes or surfaces are part of the essential creative statement, whereas it is the line that gives a drawing its life.

A travel sketch from Rome

The Tools

creative elements of drawing will also be touched upon; however, they will be discussed in more detail later in the book.

Try to approach your projects playfully; not force anything.

The first few exercises in this book introduce the tools, the different drawing surfaces, and the techniques involved in using them. Since the focus of the book is on using colored pencils, they will naturally be the most important tool that will be discussed. In addition, however, different types of eraser, pastel, oil pastel, and soft-tipped pen will be discussed, with particular emphasis on how they are used to increase the effect of the colored-pencil drawing. The

These are the basic tools.

9

The Colored Pencil

Sharpening

Many manufacturers produce colored pencils. But one of my personal favorites is Polychrome-Artist. Polychrome-Artist pencils are available in seventy-two strong colors. Their oil-chalk center creates flat, rich colors, and they won't smear, are not water-soluble, and are fade-resistant. The colors will not only adhere to paper and boards but also to acrylic fibre, wood, and textiles. Although they aren't affected by water, they can be mixed or removed with turpentine. Of particular interest to the graphic artist and designer is that this company produces five different shades between black and white.

Various companies make colored pencils that can be mixed with water, including Derwent, Mongel, Caran D'ache, Albrecht-Dürer, Steadtler Mars, and Schwan-Stabilo.

Steadtler Mars colored pencils are not only water-soluble, but they have very strong colors, which allows for a wide range of applications. They come in thirty-six different shades.

Schwan-Stabilo thin-cartridge colored pencil leaves a very sharp, precise line and the tip lasts a relatively long time. These pencils also come in thirty-six different shades, and not only do they adhere to paper but also to linen and silk.

Colored pencils lose their point rather quickly and become dull, which is similar to what happens with ordinary lead pencils. Constant sharpening is thus unavoidable. Sharpening can be done with either a pencil sharpener or a knife. The advantage of the pencil sharpener is that it creates an even tip, but the disadvantage is that the tip breaks off rather easily, particularly when pressure is increased.

An alternative to the pencil sharpener is the knife. With a knife, it is possible for the tip of the pencil to be shaped in different sizes, depending on what you want to accomplish. In general, sharpening with a knife is more economical.

I routinely sharpen my colored pencils with a knife and create different planes. Also, by rolling the pencil between my thumb and index finger while drawing, I automatically and constantly create different points and edges that I use depending on my needs. This, in addition, keeps me from having to frequently interrupt my work to resharpen a pencil, allowing me to draw lines with fluidity.

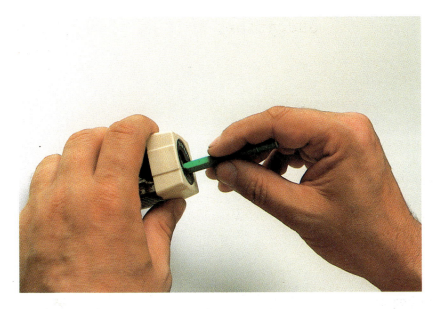

With this pencil sharpener, it is possible to sharpen pencils of different diameters simply and without problems. The small opening is for normal-size pencils; the larger for those pencils with a larger diameter. The shavings are contained in the housing, so the work space remains clean. The only disadvantage of the sharpener is that pencil tips break off very easily.

In order to avoid easy breakage of pencil tips, I use a knife, which gives me the advantage of being able to adjust the tip according to the type of line I want to draw. For larger areas, the tip is kept blunt. This saves repeated sharpening and thereby saves time; also, the pencil lasts longer.

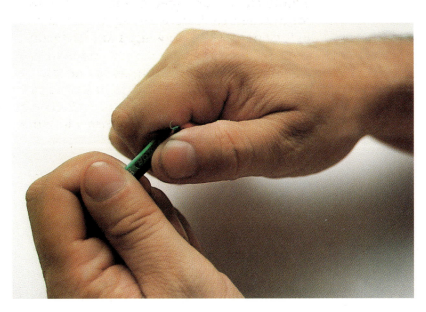

For reasons of safety, it is suggested not to sharpen a pencil with the knife moving towards one's body. However, with care and by applying only gentle pressure, this method actually poses very little danger. The advantage of sharpening towards yourself is that you have more control in creating the shape of pencil tip you desire.

Drawing Surfaces

Before embarking on your first exercises, it makes sense to become familiar with the surfaces you want to use for your drawings. In general, all surfaces made from paper and cardboard are suitable; however, your choice will depend on the effects you want to achieve.

Naturally, making the best choice requires some knowledge about the special qualities of the different surfaces available for drawing. Colors will be less intense on smooth paper than on rough surfaces, and their tone will be different. In addition, colored pencils do not adhere well to smooth paper, and a line often takes on a strained look. Other surfaces, like the rough surface of package-wrapping paper, will quickly "eat up" your colored pencils, forcing you to sharpen them constantly.

Every surface has its advantages and disadvantages, and, for this reason, it is difficult to give recommendations or specific advice. You need to experiment and allow mistakes to happen. You can learn as much from a negative outcome as from a successful one.

As times goes on, do not restrict yourself by using only colored pencils, but mix them with various water-soluble materials and practise different scratching and scraping methods to find out what kinds of effect can be created and how resilient a particular surface is. This will be very useful for future projects.

Layout paper

Smooth board

The drawing on the opposite page is based on a sketch made during a trip in the Brittany. The surface here is matt board. It was easy to expand on the original sketch by using the economical means of simple lines that nevertheless create a dense effect on the green matt surface.

In these examples, I experimented with Schwan-Stabilo (top and bottom left), Steadtler Mars (top and bottom middle), and Albrecht-Dürer (top and bottom right) pencils by drawing basic lines, cross-hatching, and creating surfaces by mixing the colored pencil with water.

Colored matt board

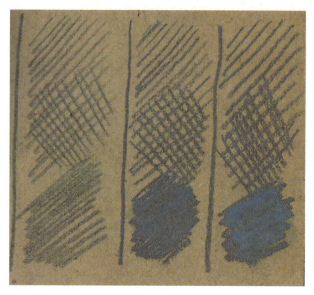

Regular cardboard

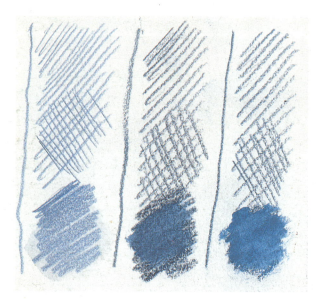

Watercolor paper

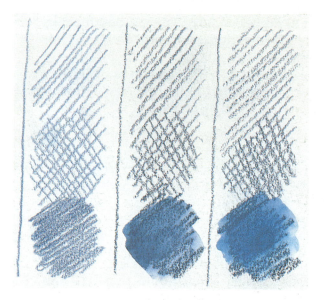

Rough cardboard or construction paper

For this drawing, entitled An Idea Takes Shape, I chose charcoal paper. It is rough, easily stressed, and tears readily when an eraser is used, but I knew that it would give me the effects I wanted.

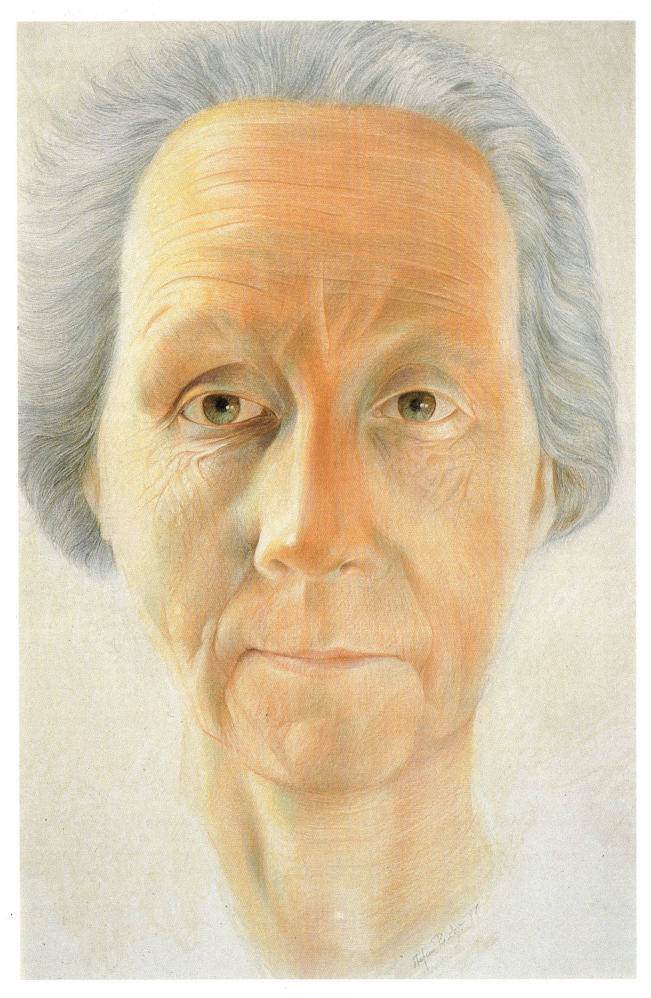

16

This drawing is a portrait of my grandmother. I used a smooth, stiff board, the same material designers often use for their finished drawings. In general, this material is not well suited to colored-pencil drawings, because colors do not adhere well to this surface and it gives a drawing a somewhat faded look. But this is precisely the effect I wanted. It allowed me to emphasize the transparency of "old" skin.

I purposely avoided abstractions, out of love for my grandmother and respect for her age. My goal was to convey the hard life my grandmother has lived, a life full of sacrifices—and I wanted to avoid any attempt to pretty her up.

As far as the technique is concerned, the soft skin tones were achieved by rubbing certain areas with a tissue, and the wrinkles and fine lines by using a very fine pencil point. For the grey hair, I used white oil pastel, scratching in the strands of hair with the tip of an X-Acto® utility knife, which made them look as they really are: soft and delicate.

Self-Portrait with Flowers

The surface for this colored-pencil drawing is a stiff, rough board, which works well to create gentle, yet grainy, pencil lines. The rough surface almost dissolves the lines so that the drawing seems to consist of many small dots.

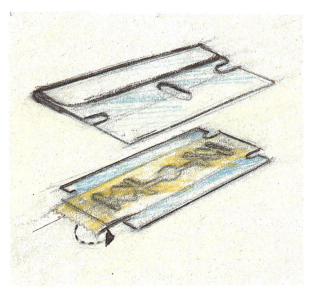

Single-edged razor blade (top) and regular razor blade, partially covered with transparent adhesive tape (bottom).

Utility knife with snap-off blade—with handle (top) and without handle, showing break line (bottom).

Tools for Scraping and Scratching

Colored-pencil drawings are not only created by adding lines but sometimes by removing traces of color, by creating light, or by lightening dark areas.

To accomplish this, you may have to erase or even scrape away some of the color already applied. Of course, this can only be done on a sturdy surface, like that of cardboard. Scraping and scratching are best done with a knife or blade, such as a scalpel or razor blade. The single-edged razor blade can be used just like a regular razor blade. But, since one side is solid, this blade is much stronger and safer to use. The razor blade has advantages over the knife because it is much more flexible. But the chance of injuries is great. To counter that chance, one cutting edge of the blade can be covered with transparent adhesive tape (see the illustration).

Another instrument that can be used for scraping and scratching is the utility knife with snap-off blades. I like to use individual blades without the handle. They can be easily broken off at the indentation, and they provide a sharp edge every time it is needed.

Fixatives

A finished drawing must be sprayed with a fixative in order to keep the colors from smudging. Today, fixatives are available in spray cans. When purchasing a fixative, make sure that it is manufactured to be environmentally safe. I usually purchase a product that can be used for both color and pencil drawings.

When, in the course of your artwork, one color has to be fixed, pastel fixative works particularly well. And clear lacquer applied to a finished drawing is ideal for creating special effects. Fixatives and clear lacquer usually are colorless. Fixatives dry to a satin finish, whereas clear lacquer creates a high-gloss finish.

Shake the spray can vigorously before applying the substance, and make sure the distance to the drawing is about 12 to 16 inches. The nozzle can be cleaned of residues by holding the can upside down and pressing on the spray head; a clogged nozzle, however, is easily cleaned with nail-polish remover.

The Graphical Means of Creating a Picture

The following exercises can be used as an introduction to the basics involved in creating a drawing. The essential elements employed in a drawing are the dot, line, and plane, as well as graphical contrasts, texture, and color.

Composition is also important. Major issues are the placement of light and dark contrasts and the strength of the motif you have chosen to work from. In terms of motifs, I recommend that you study nature, because the process of studying an object will train the eye.

A dot in the middle of a picture dominates the whole area surrounding it and creates a stable and balanced structure.

The Dot

The dot is the smallest structural element. A dot in and of itself is a complete and balanced structure. When viewed as a small plane, it can take on several different shapes, such as a circle, square, triangle, or rectangle. A dot can also appear as a small irregular spot.

When is a dot still a dot, and when does it become a plane? A dot that looks like a tiny spot on a very large surface can easily take on considerable size when placed on a 8½ × 11 inch piece of paper. However, no matter how small, this dot can make a big impact! You can experience this for yourself by putting a dot in the middle of a square. The dot will dominate. If the dot is moved away from the middle, the relationship be-

A dot anywhere outside the middle causes the relationship between the dot and the surrounding area to lose balance and stability.

tween the dot and the square immediately loses its stability.

A dot gains importance in a color drawing by the way it creates structure and texture. When many dots are placed close together, they will appear as a solid mass and can represent a plane.

Contrasts are created by randomly arranging dots of different sizes and lines.

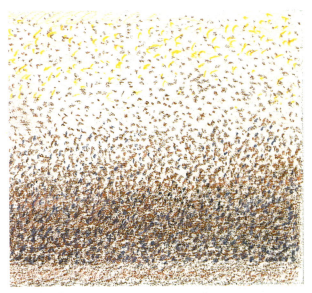

This exercise shows dots that are grouped together to create planes; however, they are not sharply defined but rather flow softly into each other.

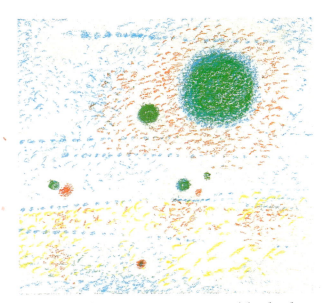

Additional contrasts are created by both small-versus-big and soft-versus-harsh dots.

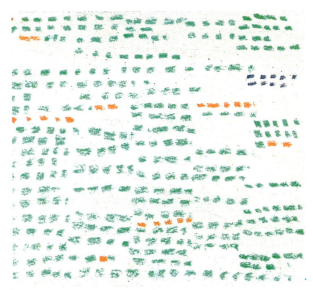

Dots grouped together in grid-like fashion create a pattern.

The effect of a solid plane can also be accomplished by shading methods. The density (or airiness) also makes it possible to simulate different values of a color.

The Line

A dot is made as soon as a pencil touches paper. A pencil moving over paper forms a line. Movement, therefore, is the characteristic of a line, which is thus dynamic by nature. A line can go in any direction: straight or curved; vertically, diagonally, or horizontally. Lines can branch out or cross each other. Lines that cross each other can take on a special function called cross-hatching. In a drawing, the line is the most important structural element.

As soon as two or more lines are present, a form is created. The space between the lines is as important as the lines themselves. This concept can be seen in the exercises that follow.

This composition consists only of lines: fine, blue vertical lines contrasted with heavier straight lines of two shades of green that are pointing in different directions.

Here, some of the horizontal lines move briefly in a perpendicular direction, creating short, vertical lines. Spaces between the lines have been filled with color.

Several triangular shapes with differing angles create a tension-filled composition.

Another possibility: lines intersecting at different angles and moving in different directions.

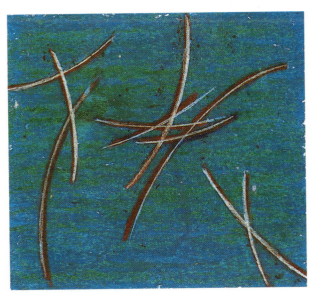

These randomly arranged curved and angled lines also create a sense of tension.

Here, some parallel lines are curved more than others; however, the overall tendency is determined by the horizontal lines.

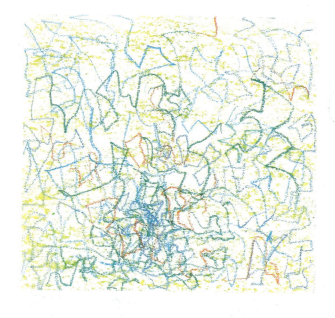

An arrangement of totally free-flowing lines, where the distance between lines is dense in some places and less so in others.

This composition, reminiscent of cells, shows lines that are branching out in different directions.

Here, lines are used to mark the boundaries of distinct forms; different forms are created by intersecting lines.

The Cathedral of Chartres—a sketch

The main element of the composition is lines. I began the drawing with a pencil and followed that with white oil pastel, which diffused the pencil lines, making them less defined. I finished the drawing with colored pencils. The soft layer of the white oil pastel made it possible for me to blend the colors in some areas; this is easily accomplished with just a finger.

This exercise is an example of an uncomplicated use of planes.

The drawing on the opposite page is a composition of different, overlapping planes. It is one of a series of ten drawings, featuring important pioneers of computer technology. The drawing shows George Stibitz developing a binary calculator at his kitchen table.

The Plane

Although you might not be aware of it, during the previous exercises you have already been introduced to the concept of "planes." For instance, at the very start we found that a dot can only function in relation to the space, or plane, in which it exists. The same is true for a line.

When we talk about the plane, we mean the space that is occupied by the picture. Kandinsky calls this space the ground, which, at the same time, determines the outside dimension of a picture. The artist can choose any shape he or she desires. In general, however the shape of a picture is rectangular.

Furthermore, we found that spaces inside a drawing, created by lines that are either connected or intersecting, are also planes. These planes are also considered shapes; they too have distinct boundaries.

In the strictest sense of the word, every dot is a plane—a very small one, to be sure, but nevertheless a plane. Planes, therefore, are shapes with definite boundaries of different sizes. When an artist draws a picture, the dot and the line are the main elements of composition; in contrast, a painter works primarily in planes. In reality, these boundaries are not always so clear, because even in a drawing the artist cannot entirely work without this basic element of composition. And sometimes a painter will use lines to give shape to a form or use dots to give texture to a composition. Pointillism (a late Impressionist method of painting) employs dots exclusively in the composition of paintings.

Relay #70 Panel F
(moth) in relay

First actual case of bug being found.

Another example: a composition of irregular, soft shapes with the look of patchlike planes. This exercise is meant to encourage experimentation.

Mountains

This drawing is also an example of how to use planes as major creative elements.

Contrasting different geometrical shapes

Here, a contrast is created by using simple geometrical shapes. They are repeated in different combinations, with the greatest contrast being between the circle and the triangle.

Contrasts of free forms

Free-form geometrical shapes are contrasted against a red background. Another, somewhat weaker contrast is created by vertical and horizontal divisions within the composition.

Graphical Contrasts

The most important graphical contrast is that of light and dark. In the chapter on composition, this subject will be discussed in more detail. But there are a number of other means of creating contrasts at our disposal. A few that might inspire your imagination are the contrast between small and large, thick and thin, straight and curved, many and few, soft and hard, and the dot and line. In the next chapter, where we deal with structure, the focus will be on those contrasts that express texture.

Contrasts give life, tension, and drama to a composition. However, they ought to be used somewhat sparingly so as not to interfere with the overall effect. Contrasts should not compete with each other; they are to serve as accents. The effect of contrasts is relative. A line will appear large or small, depending on its relationship to either a smaller or larger object. A mountain will only look massive when it is contrasted with smaller elements—for instance, with a herd of sheep. Try to make a mosquito look like an elephant by using the appropriate contrasts.

The main subject of the drawing on the opposite page is Charles Babbage, whose invention in 1822 was used to calculate mathematical formulas. The woman in the picture was working with Babbage and is considered the world's first programmer. Her image in the drawing is in contrast to the large planes in the background. Black-white is another contrast here.

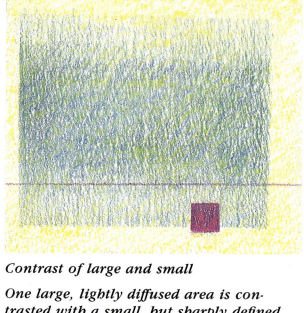

Contrast of amassment and placement of figures

The contrast in both pictures is created by the same shapes; however, they are placed differently and, therefore, give each composition a different quality.

Contrast of large and small

One large, lightly diffused area is contrasted with a small, but sharply defined, shape. The fine line heightens the tension.

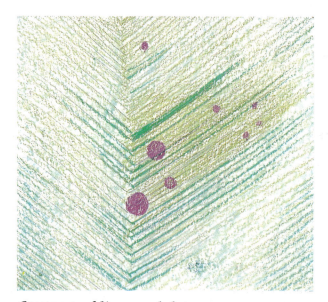

Contrast of lines and dots

Many compete with a few: lines versus dots.

Contrast of movement versus quiet

Here, lines indicating movement are contrasted with a dark square. The static figure "moves" the lines; the figure seems to float.

Contrast in direction

Many straight lines pointing in different directions give life to the whole.

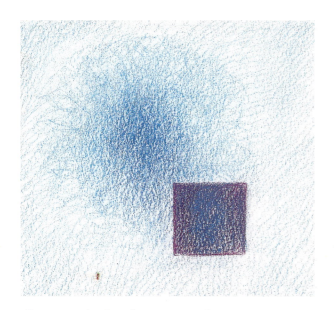

Contrast in hard versus soft

The diffuse shape in the middle gives special intensity to the square.

Contrast in direction

This creates the same effect as in the drawing above, but here the vitality is achieved with curved lines.

Texture

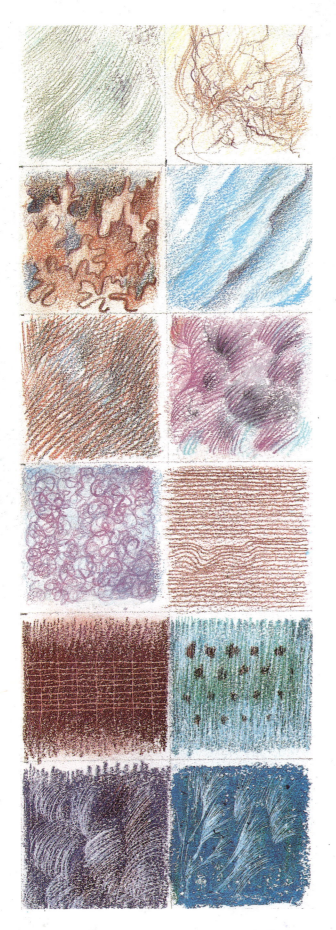

Exercises in contrast continue, but here we deal exclusively with the texture of materials, or, in other words, with surface texture. What we want to practise is creating such contrasts as the lustre of silk versus the dull texture of velvet or the firm, smooth skin of an apple versus the wilted, shrunken skin of dried fruit. But we do not necessarily have to be limited to concrete objects; we can also select abstract concepts, like fluffy versus dense.

Before you get started, put in writing what you want to accomplish and think about using the graphical tools and techniques we have discussed.

Duplicate these drawings by dividing a page into twelve squares and creating the textures as shown, adding more of your own choice if you want. The more examples you can come up with, the richer your reservoir of knowledge will be.

The Function of Color in a Composition

The world we live in is a world of color. We love the colors of meadows in spring; our mood is lifted when we look up at the deep-blue sky above us. On a grey, rainy day, on the other hand, we often are ill-humored and melancholy. Colors produce moods in people, and that is the reason why artists find working with colors so fascinating.

The Harmony of Color

While the physical properties of color are the basis for understanding the process of reproducing color in color prints and color photography, for the artist engaged in painting and drawing the primary concern is with the harmony and the psychological effect of colors. Artists have struggled throughout time with these matters.

Clouds

The object here was to create a picture by using colors only. A cloud-covered sky served as the motif. Lines going in different directions appear as cross-hatching. Contrasting colors in terms of light and dark as well as cool and warm were used to bring life to the composition; note the dark, purplish clouds in contrast to the few brightly lit areas. A rough, medium-thick Schoellershammer board was first covered with a thin layer of white oil pastel, which resulted in the soft blending of colors. The cross-hatching strokes, however, remain forceful and even. Several layers of color resulted in the overall effect.

Contrasts in Color

The general concept of contrasts in drawing and painting has already been discussed. Contrasts give life to a composition and add tension and drama. The same holds true specifically for contrasts in color. While they are only one aspect of the general theory of contrasts, they are especially important for the painter; so, for this reason, I have set aside a separate exercise section on this subject. After all, every colored-pencil drawing or painting lives because of its color—it is created with colors. The following seven categories of color contrasts were formulated by Johannes Itten, one of the teachers at the Bauhaus. They have been excerpted from his book *Theory of Harmony of Colors.*

1 Contrast from color to color

This contrast is created when pure colors are juxtaposed to each other within a painting. The addition of white and black can intensify the effect.

2 Contrast of light and dark

This contrast refers to the application of different values of color. All colors can be lightened with white and darkened with black.

3 Contrast of warm and cold

The greatest effect can be achieved with red-orange and blue-green. All other colors appear cold or warm when the shade used to create contrast is either colder or warmer.

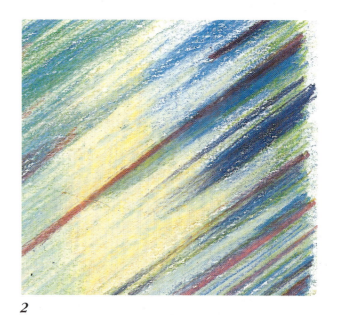

2

1

3

4 Contrast of complementary colors

Within the color spectrum, complementary colors are directly opposite each other. Complementary colors intensify when placed next to each other. Mixing complementary colors, however, results in a neutral grey-black.

5 Contrast of simulation

Every pure color psychologically demands its complementary color. If a complementary color is not present, the human eye will "create" it. For instance, strong green next to a neutral grey will give the grey a reddish tint, whereas a strong red next to grey will give the grey a greenish tint.

6 Contrast of quality

This is the contrast of brilliant versus dull colors. A color can be dulled by mixing it with white, black, grey, or its complementary color.

7 Contrast of quantity

Here, areas that differ in size and color are contrasted with each other.

4

6

5

7

Contrast from color to color.

Here, yellow, blue, and red (primary colors) as well as green and orange (secondary colors) are contrasted with each other. Every color in this example has the same degree of purity and tone.

Contrast in warm and cold

This contrast is not frequently used in drawings and paintings, which is too bad, because wonderful effects can be created, like cool shadows versus warm sunlight.

Contrast in light and dark

The intensity of this drawing does not come from the choice of colors but from the use of contrast in light and dark.

Contrast of complementary colors

Here, the complementary colors red-green, yellow-violet, and blue-orange have been purposely juxtaposed to each other.

Contrast of quality

Here are two different effects created by the "contrast of quality": In the drawing above, there is very little contrast, as the colors are similar in tone. In the drawing on the right, the yellow and red are of particular purity and brilliance in contrast to the other colors.

Contrast in quantity

The overall effect here is one of harmony, because contrasting a large area of green with a small area of red softens the contrast of both complementary colors.

Contrast of simulation

The grey in both examples is of equal intensity.

Mixing Colored-Pencil Colors

Layered shadings

You have probably already worked with watercolors. From a technical point of view, mixing watercolors is relatively simple. Any time you want to change a color, you just mix it with another color. You could, for instance, create a dull, brownish green by adding red to the green, or, by adding blue, you could create a "colder" green. This works equally well with acrylics and oil paint.

However, this principle does not hold true for colored pencils! They cannot be mixed; the colors can only be changed by layering different colors on top of each other. This makes working with colored pencils much more difficult, because you can indeed change a color, more or less as you like, but all colors naturally become darker in the process. In addition, the process of layering cannot be used indefinitely, because the ability of the drawing paper to absorb color is limited.

Layered cross-hatchings

Another way of "mixing" colored-pencil colors is to take advantage of the laziness of the human eye by setting individual colors very close to each other. It is the same system that is used in four-color prints. The finer the strokes and the closer the colors are to each other, the more perfect the deception.

The process is a little less difficult with water-soluble colored pencils. However, unlike watercolors, which are mixed on a palette or in a small dish, the colors of water-soluble colored pencils can only be mixed on the painting or drawing surface itself.

Mixed with water

This landscape drawing is a good example of layering colored-pencil colors. The colors appear gentle, light, and transparent—qualities that are best achieved with colored pencils.

The Canoe Race *was created primarily through cross-hatching, another typical way of mixing colored-pencil colors.*

The Harmony of Color in Nature

A good way to find motifs as well as study color combinations is to go out into nature. By doing this, you will develop a keen eye for natural color harmony. After you have selected a particular spot, try to duplicate as closely as possible the shades of the colors you are observing; also, try to re-create the quantitative aspect of each color present in your picture. You will notice that it is not always easy to come up with the right shade. Use a surface sufficiently large for the range of colors present; this will make your work a lot easier. In addition, try to experiment with as many different color mixtures as possible, and make use of the eraser—either to make mixing colors easier or to lighten a particular color.

After you have decided on the range of colors you need, try to compose a drawing independent from the original motif, similar to the examples on the opposite page.

I created the abstract drawings on the opposite page by taking the different color shades and values from actual motifs found in nature. Ordinary, somewhat rough drawing paper, as used here, makes shading particularly effective.

A Soccer Match

The original motif, a soccer match, has been reduced to abstractions, with the divisions in space kept intact. Blue dominates, contrasting with the red (of the person in the foreground). Emphasis is on the upward movements, from the lower left to the upper right.

The Composition of a Picture

Componere in Latin means "to put together." However, that in itself is not enough when creating a picture; we want more than that. Our goal is to combine the different elements of a picture into a harmonious whole, while still creating sufficient tension. The means artists have at their disposal are symmetry, asymmetry, concentration, or decentralizing of the theme. In addition, artists use structural elements, like lines, dots and figures—which can be employed horizontally, vertically, and diagonally—as well as curved lines and large or small areas. Furthermore, all elements from the previous exercises can also be employed, but particularly the use of contrasts and most specifically that of light versus dark.

Along with employing these various elements, every composition should have something new, be in some way original. This is what makes a piece of art distinctive and have special appeal.

This composition developed out of the bottom abstract composition on page 41. If you look closely, you can detect two people moving from left to right. However, the subject matter is only secondary because here the composition is the focal point. Similar to the drawing A Soccer Match, *on the opposite page, emphasis is on the diagonal upward movement, which serves as a contrast to the left-right movement.*

Variations on the theme "Soccer Match"

Note the differences between the compositions created with color contrasts and direction of movements. Depicting people in a drawing more concretely can also change the feeling of a composition.

Here, the symmetrical structure gives emphasis to the main object in the middle of the picture, while secondary elements to the left and right mirror each other. Symmetry gives a picture a solemn dignity, and this is why this kind of composition is often used to depict religious themes (for instance, the Madonna).

In this composition, the primary object is concentrated in the middle of the picture, with secondary elements grouped freely around it, supporting it. (Examples of this type of composition are frequently found in abstract paintings.)

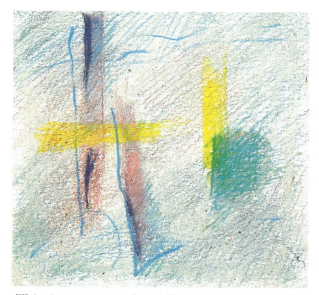

In contrast to the above, in this asymmetrical drawing the main focal point has been shifted off-center, giving life to the action.

This is an example of "decentralization," in which the main "activity" occurs off-center.

Horizontal lines create a sense of quiet. The upper portion is light and clear; below the picture becomes darker and heavier. This juxtaposition can be observed in landscape paintings, where the light or brilliance of the sky is contrasted with a sense of rootedness to the earth.

For balance, the massive figure is surrounded by smaller elements. The large object obviously dominates the scene, and this impression is intensified by its solid, black-violet color. To create contrast, the background is gentle and drawn in only soft colors.

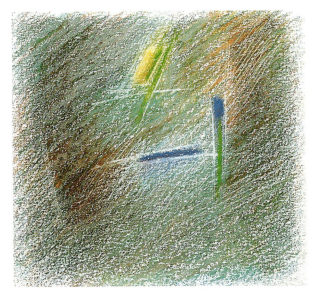

Lines depicting movements and countermovements create a sense of restlessness, threatening to burst beyond the boundaries of the drawing. To maintain a sense of equilibrium, it is necessary to determine the middle of the restless movement and provide balancing counterelements.

This drawing looks almost monochromatic, but many different colors are actually interacting with one another. Only a few small accents liven up the relatively large, greenish brown surface of the picture; This type of composition is based on the concept of more versus less.

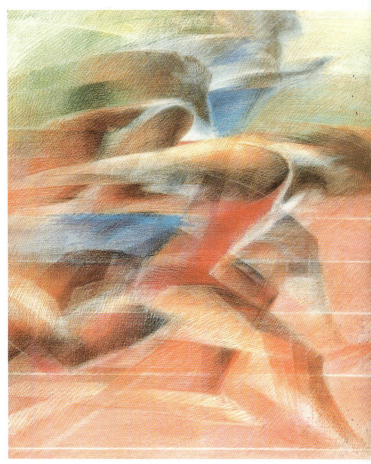

Sprinter Reaching the Goal

The main emphasis in this composition is not the people but the thrust of the ascending diagonal. The horizontal lines create contrast.

Favored elements in the composition of a picture are the use of diagonals—in both directions. That beginning at the lower left and proceeding to the upper right is called the "ascending" diagonal (top exercise); that from the upper left to the lower right is called the "descending" diagonal (bottom exercise). These terms make sense, because all figures on an ascending diagonal have an upward tendency, whereas a descending diagonal imparts the impression of falling.

Ready, Set, Go

Swimmers moving on a descending diagonal.

Dark-Light Contrast

The contrast of dark and light, or that of black and white, is a very effective creative element in drawing and painting. Take time to experiment with these contrasts. Light and dark: day and night. With this contrast alone, you can create light and shadow and three-dimensional shapes and figures.

A light-dark composition consists of light and dark dots and planes. Therefore, when you begin your picture, restrain yourself from defining shapes and figures with definite lines that you will want to fill in later. Rather, from the very beginning, create areas, or planes. This will give a picture with various color shadings—a markedly different effect from one where previously defined shapes have been filled in. In other words, a drawing that is well balanced will inevitably lose that balance within the composition as soon as areas, or shapes, are filled in with color. When concrete lines have already defined a shape, it remains unanswered whether the final shape will be light or dark.

In the top free-form composition, the light-dark contrast brings life to the action. The darker portion adds a certain depth but also a sense of mystery.

Here, the light-dark contrast is used to create the appearance of three-dimensional objects. Used severely and in an exaggerated manner, the shadows give drama to the composition while still lending the properly drawn figures an unreal appearance.

Travel Sketch from Norway

This sketch was made while riding a bus, which is the reason for the movement in the foreground. The scenery, in this case the mountains, remained "static" a little longer. Light and dark contrasts alternate throughout.

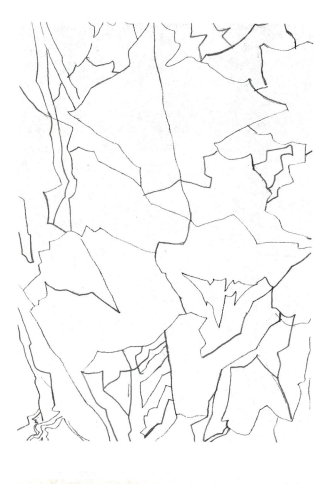

With these pencil sketches, you can see how the sharply defined shapes in the first drawing have been filled in by tinting (middle drawing) and cross-hatching (drawing on right). However, defining shapes first puts great limitations on subsequent creative work. The middle sketch shows the temptation to fill in the sharply defined areas, whereas in the sketch on the right the hatching does not quite create a unified whole.

These exercises illustrate a different approach. The first drawing was freely composed, without definite boundaries; the areas, or planes, were created spontaneously. Lines were dispensed with altogether. The middle sketch was composed in a similar fashion; however, areas, or planes, were created by cross-hatching. While cross-hatching is made up of lines, the way they are placed creates the appearance of planes. The variations in color are achieved either by varying the intensity of the lines or by layering different colors over one another. In the sketch on the right, the colored areas seem to complement each other and the free, linear structures create a unified whole. The result is a sense of movement and vitality.

Framing a Composition

With a few simple examples, you will be able to see how a "message" that a picture is conveying can be changed, depending on how the composition is framed. What a drawing is communicating can be altered according to the way an object is placed on the surface. The object can appear to pause, float, or fall; it can dominate the space or be shifted to the edge of the picture.

Your aim should be to control the space, and this entails finding the proper format for your composition. The drawing paper you choose serves as the format and determines the shape of your composition. However, you may find yourself in situations where a change of format becomes necessary, perhaps in order to shift the emphasis of your drawing. This can be accomplished by changing the way the frame is placed. For instance, an illustration for an ad that was originally intended to be printed in a vertical format may have to be changed to a horizontal format. Therefore, the ad must be reframed.

Reframing a composition can be accomplished easily with two squares, as shown. They must be larger than the picture you are working on and can be made from either white or black cardboard. These two squares can be moved over the picture until you arrive at the ideal framing. Of course, proper proportion, the relationship between height and width, must be maintained.

Partial figures

Approaching

Moving away

Positive

and negative

Isolation

The figure "melting" into the background

Figure and Ground

The partial figures play a secondary role, defining part of the composition (1). On the descending diagonal, the figures move away (2); on the ascending diagonal, they move towards the viewer (3). Placed in the middle, the figure dominates the composition. This position can be strengthened if the figure remains light and the background is darkened (4). Several figures can form a group. If one remains on the side or edge, it will convey isolation (5). When the head of a figure is in the middle of a drawing, it loses some of its dominance (6). Heavy shadows serve to add drama to the composition (7).

Dramatization through the use of shadow

The Motif

In the context of this book, "motif" is defined as a visual idea strong enough to engage the imagination, to motivate interest.

A motif can have a distinct form, be a combination of lines or colors, or be a structure. It is unimportant whether the motif was created by man or nature.

Every motif carries within itself a creative element. All you have to do is look around and be prepared to see; then every object becomes a potential motif. As soon as you detect a motif, try to think of how you can change it and which of the compositional devices at your disposal would make for the most effective drawing. However, your inspiration does not necessarily have to come from your environment. A motif can also develop from an inner vision or your imagination.

The motif (top) for the drawings (below) was chosen purposely and used as an impulse for new compositions. The drawings are dominated by several triangular shapes of varying size. Transitions from light areas to dark areas are very soft and were created with an eraser.

River Rapids in Finland

This drawing (opposite page, bottom) was originally a pencil sketch I made directly at the site where I took the photo (opposite page, top left). Later, I added color and layered the drawing partially with white oil pastel in order to achieve the hard-soft contrast.

A photo made on a trip to Finland

This drawing was made from the photo. The viewing angle was changed, and the picture was narrowed by closer framing. I coated ordinary drawing paper in white oil pastel, sketched over that with colored pencils, and then further defined the images by scratching with a blade.

Cave Steps

The two drawings on the right are examples of how an abstraction can be created from an original motif (photo, left). I chose rather rough paper for this project. It "shreds" the pencil lines, creating diffused cross-hatching; it is also well suited for soft, expansive shading. The large drawing on the opposite page is the final version.

This photo, taken on a cloudy, rainy day, really didn't turn out very well, but it is good enough to be used as a motif for a drawing.

Here, the picture conveys an entirely different mood, achieved through abstraction, the use of light colors, and a few accents.

In this drawing, the colors were effectively blended by wiping and by dragging a blade across the surface, which made the paper rough in several places. The drawing was then defined by using a sharp pencil tip. The mood, like the one in the photo, is dark and unfriendly.

In viewing only a section if this photo, the road becomes the central focus. I started by undercoating the drawing paper with white oil pastel, sketching with colored pencils, scraping with a razor blade, and then wiping with a cloth to soften the images. This left me with an airy, undefined background, on which I drew the final picture. Whenever lines were too harsh, I softened them by rubbing over them with a finger.

This photo inspired me to do a study in motion. The technique is the same as the one described on the previous page; however, I let the background remain more pronounced.

Looking for and Finding a Motif

discover new possibilities for your artwork. Trying to create a new style is a misplacement of your ambition. Instead, your aim should be to try to find the very essence of a scene or object. Do not copy an existing pattern.

The basic requirement for finding a motif is to *see consciously*. You must sharpen your awareness in order to learn how to compare and analyze. Searching for a motif takes practice. But searching will enable you to

Once you have collected material for a motif—old sketches, photos, and the like—you can then make your selection. Your imagination has no limits; the crucial factor in the end has to do with how you will have transformed the motif you chose to make it a means for your personal expression.

The motif for this illustration did not originate in nature; rather, it developed spontaneously while I was watching television. I like to make use of television-watching time because it gives me a rich variety of images to choose from and forces me to concentrate and work rapidly.

View From a Bus

This is the result of one of those spontaneous moments during a bus ride in which a motif gets lodged in my mind. I started the drawing with cross-hatching in different colors across ordinary drawing paper; next, I added a layer of white oil pastel to soften the harsh contrasts in color. Then I sketched in the telephone pole and the foreground with a soft pencil, creating a contrast in black and white.

The picture on the opposite page is an example of a totally different way of finding a motif. I made a photocopy of a photograph from a magazine, proceeded to tear it up, and then glued fragments on a board. Freehand hatching repeats the "rhythm" of the motif, creating an original, interesting composition.

Exercises in Composition

For the following exercises, eliminate the use of most other materials, and use colored pencils alone or with a little oil pastel. The choice of motif is not important here. Perhaps you can find something among the samples you already have collected, or you might want to choose a theme, like "Spring" or "Blue and Yellow." In the beginning, stick to simple motifs, because the gist of these exercises is to strengthen the techniques you have already been introduced to in the previous sections.

The first step is the choice of a format. Does your motif require a vertical or horizontal frame, or would a square be more appropriate? Next, remember to draw with a light hand and always keep in mind the total picture. A good drawing grows out of the whole. Details are attended to when the basic concept of your drawing is in place; however, even then, do not get bogged down in particulars. As with a photo that is immersed in developing solution, a drawing gains depth and power in the process of working on it. Step back from your drawing now and then and view it from different positions. Look at it sideways and upside down; this will free you from concentrating too much on the motif and allow you to see contrasts, placement of light and dark, and the balance of colors more clearly.

Shapes grow from within and their contours develop automatically. This implies that you also draw "invisible images", not necessarily with the pencil but with your eye. Try to look "behind the scene," which means that you must imagine an object in its physical state.

Roots

A clump of roots is a rewarding subject, allowing you to see all kinds of secrets in the shapes they present. In addition to brown, violet and blue can be detected in these photos.

For this exercise, begin by softly sketching with colored pencils. Then add a layer of white oil pastel, which will further soften the lines you have drawn. The drawing below was made on this type of background. Now draw your selected motif.

The drawing on the opposite page was made on layout paper. Here, too, the surface was coated with oil pastel; then details were drawn in with sharp colored pencils. Also, a considerable amount of scratching and scraping was employed.

Nature can be a wonderful motif to work from for abstract art. In this case, only the different shades and tones of the colors are important.

The last example in this section is intended as an introduction to the subject of nature studies—something very close to my heart. The sketch and photo on this page were made during a vacation. The drawing on the opposite page was finished at home. With this drawing, I tried a new technique. I first covered the surface, originally intended for working with oil paint, with tempera colors, and then I finished the drawing using traditional colored-pencil techniques.

A Plea for the Study of Nature

The wealth of shapes and colors offered by nature is inexhaustible—make use of these riches!

When studying nature, take in everything: the scenery in all its basic forms and shapes as well as all the small details. Take note of all the messages that shapes in scenery convey to you—the contrasts as well as the moods.

In the beginning, go outside and draw what you actually see; later, draw from memory. The study of an object trains your eye and increases your ability to see. Direct observation will teach you to recognize the essential characteristics that you will want to manifest in your drawing. Individual style is the result of each observer's own understanding. This, however, implies that, in order to draw, one must think and comprehend—not just copy nature, or even worse, come up with a photo-like reproduction.

Wind in Brittany

This is a drawing that began as a nature study on my vacation and was later finished at home.

The goal of a nature study, therefore, is not to replicate a motif, but rather to make visible your mental/spiritual involvement with the subject you have chosen. Only in this way will your drawing manifest a unique quality—even if you are still inexperienced—because it will be honest.

The drawings shown here are my interpretations of motifs I originally saw in nature. You should find your own style by re-creating motifs in terms of how they affect you.

This drawing is also a nature study that started as a sketch made during my travels.

This too is a "nature study"! Time and again I sit in front of the mirror, not out if vainness, but because I am a very patient model. I used a soft #4 pencil for this drawing and brown and blue Stabilo colored pencils.

Large Cathedral

This nature study was made in a forest of beech trees at a river. The motif, however, served as the basis for other images. In the course of drawing, I had a vision of a large cathedral. The tall trunks of the beech trees became columns that were supporting branches. With the sun filtering through the leaves, I had the sense of a Gothic cathedral with stained-glass windows.

Drawing Techniques

In our previous discussions on how to create a picture, our primary focus has been on graphics and composition. In the remaining sections, I would like to explain the various techniques you can use in drawing with colored pencils so that you will make as few mistakes as possible, and to send you on your way to not only becoming an accomplished artist but also one whose work conveys a sense of professionalism.

Holding the Pencil

A line with a light touch can only be produced with a light hand—a pencil held between your fingers without tension. I hold a new, little-used pencil in the middle with my thumb and index finger and let the weight of the pencil rest on the middle finger. This is the position I prefer most of the time, but especially when cross-hatching large areas.

Assessing Completion

When I work at my drawing table (elevated along its length in the back) on a large project, I like to step back periodically in order to gain an overview of my progress from a distance—something I recommend highly. It is the only way to discover when a piucture is nearing its completion and for me to know when to stop. It is all too easy, when working away industriously, to "overkill" a drawing.

Check contrasts and values by closing your eyes halfway. In low light, colors with similar values will appear to blend into each other.

Avoiding Unintentional Smudges or Blending

When making corrections in certain areas of a drawing, I cover the portions of the drawing that I don't want to disturb with a piece of paper. I also use the traditional painter's stick, on which I rest my hand so that it will not come in contact with the drawing surface. A painter's stick with cushioned ends, either with a fabric or leather, is best because it will prevent you from damaging the paper.

The lower portion of the drawing is covered with paper to protect it.

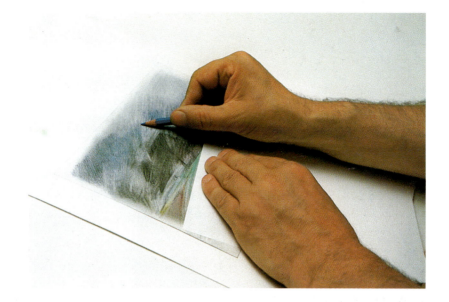

Another possibility is to work standing up, against a drawing table that is raised in the back, so that your hand is away from the surface of the paper.

Your hand can also be supported by a painter's stick. This technique has found great favor, because it allows the artist to use more pressure and makes it easier for him or her to work on fine details.

Hatching and Cross-Hatching

Hatching, whose basic element is line, and specifically cross-hatching are particularly suitable techniques for colored-pencil drawings. Hatching is similar to pointillism, which consists entirely of dots, but it is the line in the hatching technique that gives structure to a drawing.

In hatching, lines are used in a very precise and deliberate manner, as can be observed in the picture on the opposite page and those on the following two pages. Areas with lines running parallel are contrasted with those in which lines run in the opposite direction. Contrasts, therefore, are created by a change of direction. Further contrast can be created by sets of shorter and longer lines, as well as lines placed close together and others drawn farther apart.

Cross-hatching with colored pencils is a technique that works particularly well in creating colorful drawings, but especially when it come to mixing colors. Let me mention Pointillism again—a practice that developed around 1883 and grew out of the techniques used in the painting of the

Impressionist period. The Impressionists did not apply colors in a continuous manner, creating solid areas; rather, they saw colors as dots and short lines arranged in a grate-like system. It is not until the eyes of the viewer visually "mix" the dots and lines of the basic colors that differences of shades and values become apparent.

Practise hatching without the use of any other materials. Use only colored pencils. With this technique, however, corrections are almost impossible to make. You will be able to darken a drawing by intensifying the lines of the hatching, but lightening colors is not possible.

However, there is a little trick you can use by which an area that has become too dark can be softened. It is accomplished with the aid of rubber cement, a glue that graphic designers often use when assembling a montage. It is available in tubes and cans. Cover the place you want to lighten up with the glue, wait until it has dried, and then remove it. This trick is only meant to be used in an emergency—and ideally, not at all.

This drawing originated from a sketch made on a trip to the North Cape. It is useful for studying the technique of cross-hatching.

Handball: Shooting a Goal

Over the Hurdles

The drawings on these two pages are examples of cross-hatching. The colors of both drawings have been gently blended as a result of the finished surfaces having been wiped over with a tissue, which also created their soft backgrounds. Care must be taken so that the colors do not become mixed by rubbing too harshly.

Blending, Hatching, and Erasing

This exercise will give you the chance to experiment with new ways of working with colored pencils. Start your picture with light, but definite, strokes. Pay attention to only the basic structure of your drawing; details are not important in the beginning, but proper placement of planes and light and dark contrasts are. Once the overall structure is established, take a soft cloth or tissue and wipe over the entire surface.

Be very careful not to wipe those areas that you want to keep intact. To create a more compact and solid look, rub a little more. Keep in mind the total picture you want to create. Make sure that the picture does not start to look smudged, because this technique is merely intended to achieve a unified surface. Depending on your artistic intent, certain lines may remain visible.

The eraser is not only used to remove mistakes, but, at this step in the process, to create gentle transitions from one color to another or for drawing directly. When drawing with an eraser, it is best to use an eraser that can be attached to a holder.

Once the structure in its basic form is well balanced and thought through, you can begin working on fine points and details. You can now alternately use drawing, blending, and erasing until you are satisfied with your creation. In order to make your work easier, it is best to use a fixative between steps.

Up until now, we have concentrated solely on drawing with colored pencils. However, by using additional drawing materials, we can achieve totally different effects.

Wiping in light, circular motions is used for blending.

The Struggle to Possess the Ball

Here, the colors were extensively blended in order to create soft transitions.

On Your Mark, Get Set, Go
The different blues of the background were blended together and additional etching was used to achieve the soft transitions. I used an etching pen to create the fine lines.

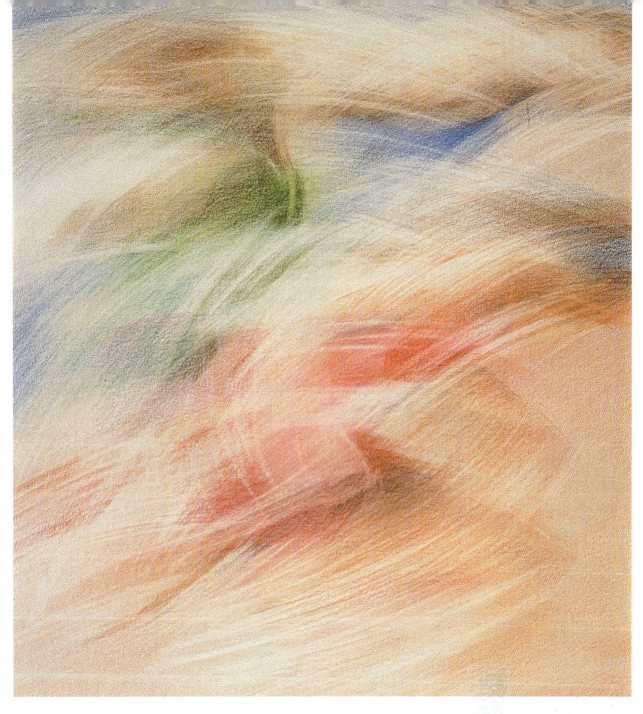

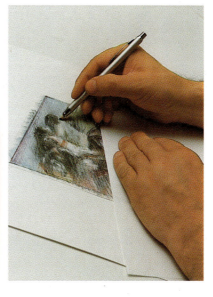

The eraser and the etching pen were used on this colored-pencil drawing. This technique is particularly effective for depicting movements in sports-action drawings.

Working with an eraser and etching pen, respectively.

Computer Landscape

The focal point of this drawing is in the middle. The computer paper looks like a road in a sparse landscape. Here, the soft transitions between the colors were achieved by blending with a tissue and an eraser.

Petra

In this drawing, areas with very dark hatchings contrast with those that are light and soft. The blouse is in harmony with the background; both are soft and transparent. The face, however, is richer in color and has much more defined contours.

In the Kitchen Door

I didn't like this picture of Petra (above). The form was too vague. It was my intention to have light partially falling on her in the door frame, but the contrast was missing. I had to completely rework the drawing (see opposite page). First, I darkened the color of the walls around the door frame; then, I adjusted the other parts of the picture. At one point, I felt the walls were too strong and dark. So, I used an eraser to lighten the colors. I left the scratching marks intact, but I softened them by applying color over them in a glaze-like fashion.

Landscape in Brittany

The surface for this landscape drawing from Brittany (28 × 20 inches) is a rough, handmade paper frequently used for watercolor paintings. This paper is very uneven and generally not well suited for colored-pencil drawings. Its characteristics, however, were just what I was looking for. The first lines on the paper looked irregular and broken up, as if they were porous. Then I applied a layer of pastels, blending the colors by continuously wiping over the surface with a soft cloth before proceeding with the next step. Colored pencils were used for the final effect; however, before proceeding with them, I covered the entire surface with a fixative.

Undercoating with Pastels

Interesting effects can be achieved in colored-pencil drawings by applying a layer of pastels, either as an undercoat or, as described on the opposite page, as an intermediate layer. While this technique requires some experience, once mastered it can be applied quickly and confidently. It makes separating areas of different colors as well as shading much easier.

Pastel colors are usually soft and easy to blend. Excess dust from the pastels can easily be blown off the surface. Since the colors are not stable, it is important to use a fixative once the process is completed. You can find pastel fixatives in art-supply shops.

Select a soft board or paper so that the pastels will adhere more easily to the surface; on the other hand, the paper should not be too soft because it also has to be able to stand up to colored pencils. If you have decided on a harder surface, do not start out with pastels, but use an indirect method by applying the pastel colors to a tissue and then rubbing them into the paper in a circular motion. I recommend being conservative when choosing pastel colors, since they are merely to serve as an undercoat, with the actual drawing beginning afterwards.

The transition between different colors can be soft or clearly defined. There is a special technique for creating distinct boundaries. You cut or tear templates, apply pastels to them with a tissue, and then place them on the surface. To avoid smudging, make sure that the pastels are fixed before proceeding.

You can apply pastels continuously using these techniques, and you can also use an eraser. But you must remember that pastels are not "blend-proof" and that your hand needs to be kept away from the drawing paper. The experienced artist works freehand, but this does not preclude the use of a painter's stick.

Cove in the Mediterranean

This picture started as a pencil drawing at the actual site and was finished at home. I layered the entire surface of the drawing with pastel colors so that the original lines could barely be made out. After applying the fixative, I drew over the drawing with colored pencils.

Undercoating with Oil Pastels

Lately, I have tended to undercoat my drawings with oil pastels, for several reasons. Oil pastels give the surface a soft, film-like coating, and the colored pencils used subsequently appear much more brilliant and sharp. Additionally, the tips of the colored pencils don't dull as fast; you can continue drawing for a much longer period without having to stop and sharpen your pencils. However, the disadvantage is that the drawing is not stable and must be handled more carefully.

Oil pastels can be bought either individually or in an assortment of seventy-two different shades (see photo). In addition to the oil pastels, you will need a regular or a single-edged razor blade, so that you can scrape particles off a stick, which can then be rubbed into the drawing paper.

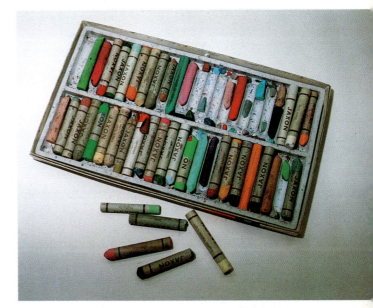

When large areas of a picture are to be undercoated, the paper covering around the sticks can be removed.

Here, the surface was undercoated with oil pastels, and soft colored pencils were used for drawing. The dominant colors are blue and black. This drawing served as an illustration to a poem, so care was taken to keep the form and mood of the composition complementary to those of the poem.

Woman in a Mirror

Harsh, wide cross-hatching stands in contrast to portions that are softly blended, where traces of the oil pastels were rubbed into the paper. The composition also comes alive through the cold-warm contrast created by the reddish highlights in an arrangement of otherwise cool, greenish blue shades.

Clouds

For the surface of this drawing, I chose a rigid, rough board, which I covered with white oil pastel. I used soft colored pencils and blended the colors with the oil pastel. For this drawing, I used the cross-hatching method, over the undercoating. (This drawing has already appeared in the book to illustrate other points.)

Mixing Colored Pencils with Water

As mentioned earlier, Derwent, Mongel, Caran D'ache, Stabilo, Steadtler Mars, and Albrecht-Dürer pencils are all water-soluble.

The solubility differs among them, however, so experiment to see which ones will suit particular projects. But the difference in solubility says nothing about the quality of their results. For instance, the poor solubility of the Stabilo pencil can actually be very useful, because more details of a drawing will stay intact when the whole drawing is treated with water. In contrast, the Albrecht-Dürer colored pencils are totally soluble. This implies that the best pencil to choose is up to the artist. In addition to the colored pencils, you also need watercolor brushes, a piece of cloth, and a glass of water. A sponge can also be very useful, but it is not absolutely necessary. Do not skimp when buying a brush; the best are the ones made from red marten hair. On the other hand, for the water, a used jelly or jam glass container is sufficient and, for the cloth, an old rag will do.

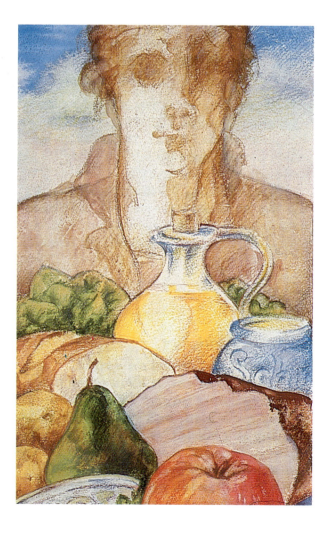

Scraping and Scratching

Whereas the beginning exercises essentially called for colored pencils only, you can now build on those basics by adding blades and, if you think it necessary, an eraser. For scraping, I like to use regular or single-edged razor blades; for scratching, I prefer to use the narrower blade of an X-Acto knife—that used to cut out templates. With these tools, you will be able to add structure and contours to your drawings. Contours will appear white, unless they are colored in soft shades later on.

The technique is best explained if you look at the drawing on the opposite page, *Self-Portrait with Smoky*. There are many different objects in this drawing: plants and butterflies, a self-portrait, a hand holding a pencil, and a black-and-white cat. Each of these objects has its own shape and surface structure, which all have to be created without diminishing the overall impression.

Therefore, the first step is to create a precise sketch. Small corrections can always be made, but the overall concept cannot be altered.

For this drawing, I chose a 4R-board from Schoellershammer, because it is strong and resists damage; in other words, it won't be harmed when blades are used.

The drawing was started in a normal fashion. I first worked with light strokes, outlining large shapes. Next, I added the details until all the shapes of the drawing were in place. Only then did I start to work with the blade, to begin the fine work. I carefully gave structure to the shapes, working on one section at a time, always keeping in mind what I wanted the finished picture to look like.

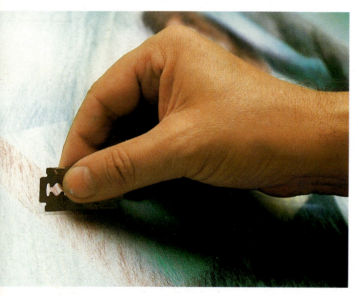

Scraping with a razor blade

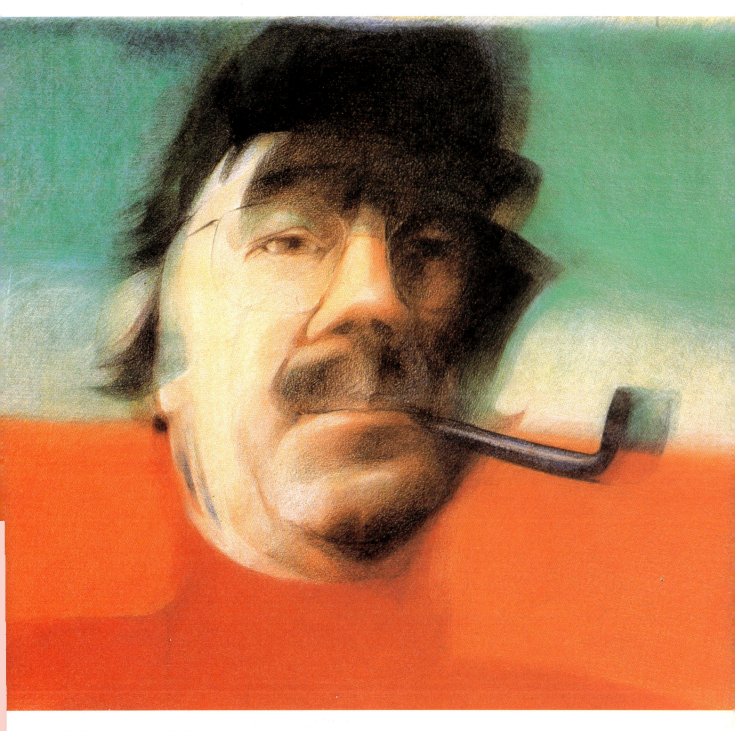

Self-Portrait with Pipe

This picture was drawn on a rigid, slightly rough board. It allowed me to apply strong colors, so that I could subsequently use a blade and do as much scraping as I needed. Part of the color pigment, however, was absorbed by the board, which produced an overall shadowy effect. After this process, the board lost its rough surface and became nearly *as smooth as a mirror. I then continued working on this smooth surface. This method took a lot of time, which was justified, however, by the rich shading of the finished picture.*

Mixing Colored Pencils with Water

As mentioned earlier, Derwent, Mongel, Caran D'ache, Stabilo, Steadtler Mars, and Albrecht-Dürer pencils are all water-soluble.

The solubility differs among them, however, so experiment to see which ones will suit particular projects. But the difference in solubility says nothing about the quality of their results. For instance, the poor solubility of the Stabilo pencil can actually be very useful, because more details of a drawing will stay intact when the whole drawing is treated with water. In contrast, the Albrecht-Dürer colored pencils are totally soluble. This implies that the best pencil to choose is up to the artist. In addition to the colored pencils, you also need watercolor brushes, a piece of cloth, and a glass of water. A

sponge can also be very useful, but it is not absolutely necessary. Do not skimp when buying a brush; the best are the ones made from red marten hair. On the other hand, for the water, a used jelly or jam glass container is sufficient and, for the cloth, an old rag will do.

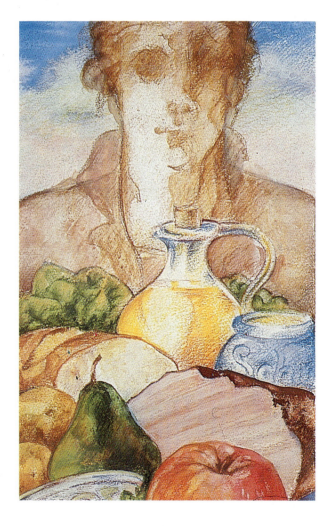

This drawing was created for a brochure. Here, I chose Stabilo pencils. After its completion, I carefully went over the drawing with a brush. I placed a piece of paper on top of the still wet drawing, stroking it with the palm of my hand. An interesting pattern resulted when the paper was removed.

Houses in Brittany

The colors of the Albrecht-Dürer pencils are completely soluble in water, so I made use of this characteristic for this picture. In order to enhance the scenic effect, I chose watercolor paper. The colors were first dissolved with a large #10 watercolor brush and then more colors were added to the wet picture. The line of the colored pencil turned out to be very soft as a result of the water. However, an advantage of using colored pencils instead of watercolors is that the texture of the dissolved colored-pencil line remains unchanged throughout the process.

Combining Colored Pencils with Soft-Tipped Pens

Colored pencils and soft-tipped pens can be used together in different ways. For instance, the colors of the colored pencils can be dissolved with those of the soft-tipped pens. Soft-tipped pens, including the broad-tipped layout pens, allow you to quickly create large areas in a composition. Drawing and detailed work are undertaken afterwards. However, you can also work in reverse: Complete the drawing first and use the soft-tipped pens as the concluding step.

In spite of all the different soft-tipped pens available, in practical terms it is wise to limit yourself to one or two brands. Of course, it goes without saying that you need to check beforehand which ones will meet your requirements. Some manufacturers offer up to two hundred different shades. Know your specific needs when choosing among different brands; it will save you money.

Both of these techniques can be varied by using water-soluble or -insoluble colored pencils. In the same way, your choice of soft-tipped pen also plays a role in the outcome of your work. There are many types of soft-tipped pen on the market, which is why I will refrain from mentioning any specific ones. The only deciding factor in choosing a soft-tipped pen is that it be one that is not water-soluble.

Time Disappearing

The surface for the drawing on the opposite page is thin layout paper, meant to be used with soft-tipped pens. I first used colored pencils and then followed that by moving a broad, layout soft-tipped pen across the drawing in quick strokes. The faster you move across the drawing, the less the colors will dissolve.

A Green Bug

Here, too, the colored pencil should be water-soluble. I used a thin soft-tipped pen, creating one dot at a time. In this way, the drawing began to glow.

Both of these pictures started out as pencil drawings. In the landscape sketch, the color of the colored pencil is more intense, while in the architectural drawing, colored pencils were used much more sparingly. In both cases, the color remained monochromatic, blue-grey being the dominant color.

Coloring a Graphite-Pencil Drawing with Colored Pencils

A pencil line has a metallic sheen that is not quite in harmony with the rough, grainy line produced by colored pencils. This contrast can be softened by spraying the finished work with lacquer. Once the picture is framed and behind glass, the lacquer is almost undetectable.

However, pencils do have a few specific advantages. Pencils don't have to be sharpened quite as often as colored pencils, and they are available in many different grades of hardness or softness.

Each graphite center produces its own shade of grey, which can be varied according to the pressure applied to the pencil. A pencil drawing can consist of an endless array of only grey shades.

From my experience, I have found that colored pencil within a pencil drawing should be used only very sparingly. This holds true for the intensity as well as the number of colors. In other words, if several colors are added to a drawing, the strength of the colors is lessened; if more intense colors are your goal, the colors that are used should be applied very deliberately and only in a few places.

In the section on "Contrasts in Color," we talked about the contrast of quantity. The overall effect will be one of harmony when *much* (in this case, the grey of the pencil lines) is contrasted with *less* (here, the color).

Thoughts of Revenge

This is an illustration for a story in which a prisoner is fixed on taking revenge on his girlfriend. The lines in the picture were made solely with grey and blue colored pencils. Although they are in harmony, they still stand in light-dark contrast to each other. A photo of the girlfriend, which has been blended into the picture, serves as a contrast to the drawing of the prisoner.

Combining the Technique of Collage with Colored-Pencil Drawing

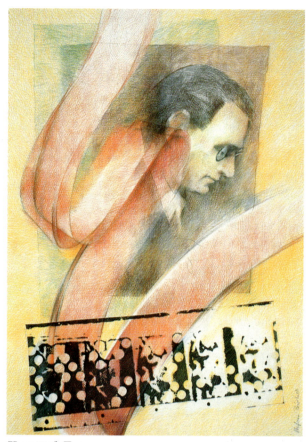

Very interesting pictures can be created when the colored pencil is just one of the "tools" used in a composition and if the concept of a "drawing" is not interpreted too narrowly.

In order to inspire your imagination and expose you to new techniques, look at this collection of colored-pencil pictures, some of which also include photographs assembled in the form of collages.

Konrad Zuse

Gottfried Wilhelm Leibnitz

Blaise Pascal

*Philipp Matthäus
Hahn*

All four of these portraits of famous mathematicians and forerunners in the computer field were made by combining colored-pencil drawing with other elements, such as photos and graphical patterns. Portions of some are the result of putting paper over a grate or other relief-like material and rubbing a colored pencil over it until a pattern became visible on the paper.

The separately prepared sections were cut out and then arranged on a different piece of paper, to which drawings were then added. Cross-hatching and empty spaces, as well as layers of color, are the building blocks of these pictures.

Possible Uses for Colored-Pencil Illustrations

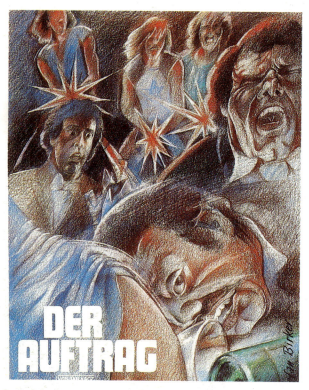

*The Order (*Der Auftrag, *in German)*

An illustration for a novel, this drawing was made on a stable, rough board with Stabilo pencils. After drawing, contours and details were scratched in with a single-edged razor blade. This is what makes them appear white. In addition, the white lines that are spread over the entire drawing bring harmony to the colors.

Visual Support

Illustrations have long been used to enhance literary works, magazine articles, newspaper reports, and advertising—in other words, whenever a text is in need of further, visual support. Whereas a drawing stands on its own, an illustration is always connected to a text.

The function of an illustration may vary, depending on the reason it is being used. Illustrations can enhance, support, or explain; it all depends on what they are intended to accomplish. In the context of this book, we are only interested in illustrations made with colored pencils. Several different types of illustration will be presented on the following pages.

The drawing on the opposite page also represents visual images from a novel. It does not depict one particular scene but rather is a condensation of the most important events in the story. The colors are muted, almost monochromatic, being brown and brown-related. The drawing technique was restricted to simple methods. As with many of the previous pencil drawings, a rough drawing surface was used.

Die Bremer Stadtmusikanten (The Town Musicians of Bremen)

The three sketches and two finished pictures on these pages are illustrations for a fable. You determine for yourself which of the two finished versions you like best. I used soft colored pencils because they allowed me to draw with broad strokes. It was important to have the brightly lit window contrast well with the dark, starry night sky, but, at the same time, to keep the animals from being swallowed up. That's why I used almost no color when I drew the animals.

The Gothamites

For this fable, I created two variations of the same theme. When the Gothamites built their town hall, they forgot to put in windows. So, they are shown stumbling into a dark room; later, they tried to carry light into the town hall in sacks and pots. In the first picture, contrasts are somewhat fuzzy; in the second version, they are much more distinct, yet the overall impression is still somewhat abstract.

Scientific Illustrations

The prerequisite for scientific illustrations is and always has been technically good and clean drawing, based on the study of nature. More than anybody else, the artists of the Renaissance are proof of how much the study of nature can turn into scientific endeavors. They were the ones who invented the technique of perspective, and it was Leonardo da Vinci who acquired botanical and anatomical knowledge while studying and intensely observing nature. In order to make abstract knowledge visible, the artist must know and be able to visualize the subject matter. Only then will it be possible to transform this knowledge into visual images.

But scientific drawings must also be reproducible, and that creates some problems for colored-pencil drawings. The main reason is that the grainy texture of the drawing intensifies on film. However, if the colored pencils are employed properly and with skill, colored-pencil drawings can be a welcome addition to this genre.

Bug

Here, a soft-tipped pen, point for point, dissolved the drawing made with Stabilo pencils and gave the drawing more luminescence.

Beech-Tree Caterpillar

This caterpillar has little in common with the other members of the species. The last pairs of legs are thick, resembling the ends of a branch. Both pairs of front legs are elongated, which is very unusual for a caterpillar. The smaller drawing shows an interim state in the drawing process, with the middle portion in particular being unfinished; it can serve as an example of how I approach this kind of illustration. This drawing has been made solely with colored pencils. Only a few small portions have been touched with a fine brush and water in order to give depth to the illustration.

Fashion Illustrations

The following examples show how colored pencils can be used for fashion illustrations. Fashion illustrations call for a special way of drawing figures. The clothes, not the figure, are the important elements in the drawing. This and the ideas of the designer are what have to be emphasized.

A conspicuous characteristic of fashion illustrations is the elongation of the human figure. It is a trick to make the clothes look more appealing. For the same reason, the models are thin and tall. It is very important that fashion illustrations be flowing and express lightness. Essentials are highlighted; unimportant details are left out. The colored pencil almost seems to be made for this kind of drawing, either used for the entire drawing or for adding color and life to an otherwise black-and-white illustration.

For these illustrations, photocopies were made of the original drawings, and they in turn were filled in or highlighted with colored pencils. In order to give "bounce" to the illustrations, outer contours in some cases were ignored.

The Caricature

For a cartoon drawing, what is most important is to convey an idea with as few lines as possible. This requires a high degree of skill in observation and the ability to get to the heart of a situation. The caricature gets its life from exaggeration and humorous representation.

Studying nature is also extremely important for a caricaturist. However, from nature only supplementary images can be borrowed that will be useful in expressing the caricaturist's own ideas.

Here are a few examples that show how effective colored pencils can be when it comes to drawing caricatures.

These frog caricatures were made specifically for a slide presentation and were only intended to lighten it up.

How Do I Catch a Crocodile?
This is an illustration for a book.

Foreclosure

The European Court

Competition Among Salespeople

Inheritance

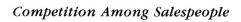

. . . and now I wish you luck with your own artwork.

Index *Illustrations indicated by an "f"*